From Your Servant's Heart

Poems Expressing Love and Adoration for Jesus

Rosetta H. Johnson

WestBow
PRESS
A DIVISION OF THOMAS NELSON

Scripture taken from the King James Version of the Bible.

WestBow Press books may be ordered through booksellers or by contacting:

WestBow Press
A Division of Thomas Nelson
1663 Liberty Drive
Bloomington, IN 47403
www.westbowpress.com
1-(866) 928-1240

ISBN: 978-1-4497-2465-8 (e)
ISBN: 978-1-4497-2466-5 (sc)

Library of Congress Control Number: 2011915526

Printed in the United States of America

WestBow Press rev. date: 9/23/2011

A Tribute to My Family and Friends

His to Keep

I know that Jesus loves me
All my life, I have heard
I have no reason to doubt it
Because I have read it in His word

Who else would die on the cross
To give life to a sinner like me
In fact, no one else could
Set all the captives free

I claim membership in the royal family
A peculiar people to some
I am a member of a chosen generation
Serving a God who is above everyone

He is my personal physician
And He heals all my pains
He provides all my needs
Everything He says sustains

He gave me the gift of life
And a beautiful world to enjoy
I have all the reasons to love Him
In Him I find true joy

I love the Lord
He knows my heart
I continue to sin
Yet, He gives me a fresh start

He knows my likes and dislikes
All my wants and deep desires
He knows my inner thoughts
And everything that I admire

He knows if I am faithful
He knows if I tell a lie
He knows everything about me
There is nothing that I can hide

He is a God that is kind and gentle
He is caring, loving and just
He commands me to worship Him only
There is no other option, it is a must

He smiles with me when I am happy
He comforts me when I am sad
He upholds me when I am weak
He is always there, and I am glad

When I attempt to think of the mystery of God
My finite mind does not comprehend
I open my heart to receive Him
And welcome Jesus to enter in

What would I do if Jesus were not there
No one to listen or hear my prayers
I would live and not have life
Living in misery and strife

I cannot let Him go
My heart is in too deep
He is my Lord and Savior
I am His to keep.

God bless you,

Rosetta Johnson

Contents

Foreword

I have known Rosetta for many years. From the time we were first acquainted, I could see that Rosetta possessed a quintessential passion for excellence in all that she pursued. She exudes a precise, dedicated tendency towards her family, friends, and career. Therefore, it comes as no surprise that she would want to charismatically share with others *From Your Servant's Heart*.

This book will take you on a journey of discovery and provide you with much unparalleled enlightenment. You will engage in the unique discovery of the varied secrets held in the hearts of man. With the turn of each page, you will be touched by heartfelt, inspirational passages.

When I think back on the relationship I have shared with Rosetta, I can say I am grateful that God has granted me the privilege of being graced by her friendship, encouragement, and unwavering support. To know her is to love her. Knowing her has brought many bountiful blessings my way.

To the lives of many, she has brought joy, hope, and opportunity. She has been divinely endowed with the rare ability to assist in opening doors and lighting paths for those in her midst. She instills within others the tenacious disposition of pursuing life to the fullest and never taking "NO" for an answer. Just know that by reading this thought-provoking book, you will be uplifted and forever changed.

Venita McCrea Cannon,
Writer & Entrepreneur

Preface

From Your Servant's Heart is a collection of poems written over a period of several years. I was inspired to write these poems in various settings: from sitting on the choir while my choir mate, Jackie Brooks, read what I was writing; to gazing at the blue waters in Aruba; to reading scriptures in my Bible or listening to my pastor while he delivered Sunday morning messages; to watching TV evangelists or late at night while lying in bed. Sometimes just thinking about people dear to me or just reflecting on my own life sparked an inspiration for a poem.

Several of the poems are quite lengthy, but I wrote the poems according to how I was feeling or what I was thinking about at that time. Two of the poems were written specifically for my two girls. When I wrote the poem titled "My Valentines," I was thinking of how gracious God had been to me in allowing me to birth two beautiful girls and how they had grown into young ladies. I was not focusing on their physical beauty, which we parents see; but on their inner beauty from my spiritual eyes. My deep love for them is nothing compared to the love God has for them.

I wrote the poem titled "Captain Carla Renee' Johnson" to give to my daughter to take with her to Iraq in 2009. I wanted to express my love for her and at the same time, give her hope of having divine protection while she was away in a distant land. As a soldier, she never expressed fear of her mission, but I think soldiers are conditioned mentally for such situations. Nevertheless, I felt this deep yearning to express in a way that I knew she would relate and give her the reassurance that God's protection was over her life. She was instructed to not read this particular poem until she was actually in the sky in route to Iraq. In fact, I gave her the un-edited copies of all my poems to take with her to read. She told me later that the poems made her cry. To me, that meant she was deeply touched within her spirit.

I organized the poems and asked a few of my friends to read them and express their thoughts. Venita Cannon told me I needed to have them published. Eyvette Johnson said likewise. Betty Stephens said they are heart-warming and actually got permission to use the reunion poem for her recent class reunion. Ernestine Middleton said that the poems ministered to her soul and suggested the title of the book. Madelene Chandler told me the poems were inspiring and great to read. She also said that people who write poems that rhyme want to be 'perfect.' Well, that pretty much describes me.

Madelene is a dear friend of mine who is currently residing in a nursing facility. I expressed to her my desire to have the poems recorded on a CD and distributed to people confined in such facilities. In fact, that was the initial concept of this project. I went to the extent of soliciting a friend, Maxcine King, to practice reading the poems for recording. I never seriously considered a book until my dear friend, Lou Stewart, suggested I do both. I have taken the first step, the book. Next is the CD.

My prayer is that these poems will bring hope and enlightenment to whatever situation one may be dealing with. I trust you will enjoy reading the poems as much as I enjoyed writing them. I pray God will continue to inspire me to write poems that encourage and inspire the hearts of others.

From Your Servant's Heart

**Poems Expressing Adoration
and Love for Jesus**

Rosetta H. Johnson

Knowing that Christ being raised from the dead dieth

no more; death hath no more dominion over him.

Romans 6:9

Not Guilty

Lord, you never plead guilty
No wrong have you ever done
You took away all our sins
When you died on Calvary and won

I will tell the story of you, Jesus
And your death upon the cross
How you paid the price for all of us
Preventing our souls from being lost

To Be Like Jesus

All our sins, Jesus has washed away
No debt we had to pay
We have the freedom to worship Him
Each and every single day

God's image must shine through us
Bidding lost souls to the cross
Being a disciple for Jesus
Sharing the gospel to all who are lost

To be with Jesus
Talk with Him in your daily prayer
Allow him to be in your presence
And have a peace of mind knowing He is there

Rosetta H. Johnson

He that dwelleth in the secret place of the most high shall abide under the shadow of the Almighty. I will say Lord, he is my refuge and my fortress; my God; in Him will I trust.

Psalm 91:1-2

God's Grace

Every moment God keeps watch
His grace and mercy continue to sustain
Never stop giving Him honor
Proclaim His glory and praise His name

Dwell in the secret place of His presence
Be attracted to Him like the fragrance of a flower
Solemn peace He will give to you
With the awesomeness of His glorious power

What a joy it is to be in His presence
Proclaiming His gospel first-hand
Being a mouth piece for Jesus
Following God's Holy commands

Seeing ye have purified your souls in obeying the truth
through the Spirit unto unfeigned love of the brethren, see
that ye love one another with a pure heart fervently.
1 Peter 1:22

My Valentine

Valentine, Valentine, I am referring to you
Mama's little sweethearts so pure and so true
I asked God to bless you and keep you in His care,
Follow God's examples and your burdens He will bear

Be mindful of His teachings
Practice what He says
He will never leave you
All of your days

My Valentine, My Valentine,
You know how much I love you
Almost as much as Jesus
Who can make all your dreams come true

Redeemed

I thank God for the many blessings
He has given to me
For life, health and strength
And the gift of eternity

He watched over me last night
As I lay in my bed asleep
I was awakened early this morning
With plenty of food on my table to eat

My love for Jesus clings deep in my heart
A passion I do not understand
I am your obedient servant
Attempting to keep your holy commands

I thank you for your unconditional love
Interceding for me through the Father from above
Keep me humble with a pure heart and mind
Blessing me with your wisdom—one of a kind

Rosetta H. Johnson

> *And the angel said unto to her, Fear not Mary, for thou hast found favor with God. And, behold, thou shalt conceive in thy womb, and bring forth a son, and shalt call his name Jesus.*
> ### *Luke 1:30-31*

The Birth of Jesus

I love the Christmas story
Of Jesus' birth on earth
The precious gift given to mankind
Who did not understand His worth

He was born of the Virgin Mary
Overshadowed by the Holy Spirit
Slept in a lowly manger
Kept free from any danger

He left the glories of Heaven
To become a humble servant on Earth
Raising us above our dreadful situation
Fulfilling the purpose given to him at birth

Reconciliation to God

Because of what God has done in my life
I am God's new creation in Christ
Old things are passed away
My new way of living begins today

I will study the Gospel
Making sure I understand the Word right
I will not get caught in the darkness
Like a child lost at night

God made provisions to grant me reconciliation
For me, there will never be another separation
I will serve you forever
In the sunshine or the stormy weather

Teach me to love you more
My love for my brothers will soar
I will stay in fellowship with thee
My inner spirit now agrees

I am thankful for all the blessings of this world
My deep love for you I long for more
When I examine my inner self
You are the one I truly adore

You always pick me up when I fall
And you provide the resources to make me right
The joy you give is my real strength
I am no longer in darkness, but shining in the light

8

Withhold from me your wrath
Don't let me perish in my sins
I give you all the praise and the honor
You said you would always be my friend

For I have received of the Lord that which also I delivered
unto you, that the Lord Jesus the same night in which he
was betrayed took bread; and when he had given thanks,
he broke it, and said take, eat; this is my body, which
is broken for you; this do in remembrance of me.
1 Corinthians 11:23-24

The Bread of Life

Jesus you are the bread of life
I have never missed a meal
It is available to me daily
I bow my head, pray and kneel

God my Christ and the center of life
I humbly accept your will
It is through your grace and mercy
My desires are fulfilled

I can do nothing on my own
I do not have the will or the power
You are the bread of life
Let me feast on it every hour

I am incapable of giving life to myself
Only you can give new birth
In spite of all my sinful ways
You still accept me for what I am worth

Rosetta H. Johnson

But the fruit of the Spirit is love, joy, peace,

longsuffering, gentleness, goodness, faith.

Galatians 5:22

Focused

Keep me ever, always focused
Never blinded with my mind
Let my eyes be centered solely
On the spiritual fruit of many kind

Peace, joy and happiness
A few of the sweets I enjoy
Your faithfulness and gentleness
Everyday I must employ

Keep me ever, always focused
On eternal things of life
Never concerned about tomorrow
Free from worry and from strife

And God said, Let us make man in our image, after our likeness; and let them have dominion over the fish of the sea, and over the fowl of the air, and over the cattle, and over all the earth, and over every creeping thing that creepeth upon the earth. So God created man in his own image, in the image of God created he him; male and female created he them.
Genesis 1:26-27

God's Image

The image of you God
Let it reflect through me
Through my actions, works I do
Things that will last for eternity

Never blinded with my eyes
Fixated on self or other things
Being darkened to your promises
Recognizing the gifts you bring

Lift the veil from my eyes
Let your light shine through
Allow the makeup of your team
Include me in the chosen few

Your presence I will feel
Knowing your face will be revealed
You are my hope and my glory
Let my actions tell your story

I am available to you
Tell me what you want me to do
Make me listen to your instructions
Making sure there are no interruptions

My hope is set on only you
Because I know your word is true
Keep the veil lifted from my eyes
Keep me safe and not easily disguised

Transform me into your likeness
Let others see Christ through me
Let the world know I am your disciple
Standing on your truth makes me free

But made himself of no reputation and took upon him the form of a servant and was made in the likeness of men.

Philippians 2:7

The Humble Servant

Jesus, Jesus, our Heavenly king
Came to this world in an humble way
His purpose was to die for our sins
That we may serve Him every day

He teaches us to be humble
To serve others genuinely from our hearts
Each day He grants us brand new mercy
From Him how can we ever depart

Seek spiritual freedom
The freedom only Christ can give
Love, hope, joy and peace
An eternal home where we can live

Rosetta H. Johnson

Behold, I stand at the door and knock, if any man hear my voice, and open the door, I will come in to him, and will sup with him, and he with me.

Revelation 3:20

The Door Swings Open

God's church has opened doors
To all who wish to enter
He searches the hearts of all the faithful
And cautions us not to linger

I know your desire is for your people to be one
Your plan is not to divide
But to work hand in hand for a common good
And you promised to be by our side

I may fall short of your expectations
And revert to my ungodly ways
Because you are a just and merciful God
You forgive me, and I give you the praise

Why you love me so much, I will never know
Question You! I will never ask
Praise and honor I give to you
And try to love you back

Let not your heart be troubled, you believe in God, believe
also in me. In my Father's house are many mansions, if it were
not so, I would have told you. I go to prepare a place for you.
And if I go and prepare a place for you, I will come again,
and receive you unto Myself, that where I am, there you may
be also. And whither I go ye know, and the way ye know.
John 14: 1-4

Citizenship

My citizenship is in Heaven
From which I eagerly seek the Savior
I know my Lord is waiting for me
I will not linger nor belabor

One day at a time I will seek His face
Letting His words dwell in my heart
Waiting patiently as a citizen
Never letting the joy in my heart depart

I will hold on to His promises
Expecting great things along the way
Through prayer and supplication
Worshiping God every day

I belong to one body in Christ
God will not let me stumble
I am a member of one household
He will always keep me humble

Watching God's goodness and mercy unfold
I belong to a chosen people, by God himself you see
I am at peace with the Lord
There is nothing that can harm His spirit in me

                        Rosetta H. Johnson

*For God so loved the world, that he gave his
only begotten Son, that whoever believeth in him
should not perish, but have everlasting life.*
John 3:16

My Eternal Home

When I have reached the end of my earthly journey
And come knocking at Heaven's door
Welcome me with open arms
My tears of joy will overflow

Help me Lord to keep the faith
To continue to put up a good fight
When life on Earth is over for me
I can tell family and friends good night

I will keep the faith and
Always believe in God's Son
When my life on Earth is finished
Into Heaven I will run

Let my daily life show others
The Jesus in me I profess
As I walk into the gates of Heaven
My Savior will say, welcome my child, be blessed

Then said Jesus to those Jews which believed on him, if ye continue in my word, then are ye my disciples indeed; and ye shall know the truth, and the truth shall make you free.

John 8: 31-32

I Am Free

Jesus went away to prepare a place for me
Where my soul, one day, will be set free

Salvation you gave to all
We only need to heed your call

Heaven is where we will take our final rest
After we have passed all the earthly tests

Living more and more like you each day
Following you daily all the way

Never losing faith and keeping a joyful heart
The Holy Spirit within us will never depart

We glorify your name for dying on Calvary
Your death gives me hope for eternity

Rosetta H. Johnson

> *It is a fearful thing to fall into the hands of the living God.*
>
> *Hebrews 10:31*

God's Faithfulness

It is a fearful thing to fall
Into the hands of the living God
His wrath, I cannot imagine
If my name, by chance, He calls

I am so glad that God is faithful
And my faith is not built on me
Though I have sinned, I'm redeemed because of God
Only His Holy eyes can see

A little spark of God's love
Can ignite within me a fire of happiness
For me to love God more
And receive His eternal blessedness

O yes, I love Jesus
Because He first loved me
I will serve none other
None other than Thee

God's Righteousness

Whatever you do
Do it for God's glory
So others may see God
As you visibly tell the story
Seek God first
Never have any doubt
Whatever you do
Everything else, He will work out

The seeking of God
Is for everyone
The way we live, pray or
Even have fun
God's righteousness is free
An expensive price He paid
Stay connected to believers
You will never be afraid

Be saved from this perverse generation
Set your mind on Holy thoughts
Be steadfast and unmovable
Emulate the lifestyle God taught
Stay connected to the body
Come to prayer meetings
Wear a cheerful smile
And have a pleasant greeting

Rosetta H. Johnson

Draw near to God
With conviction in your heart
Because of what He has done
You have a new start
God is our high priest
Whose presence is there all the time
He is a loving God
His spirit surpasses all mankind

Then we which are alive and remain shall be caught
up together with them in the clouds to meet the Lord
in the air, and so shall we ever be with the Lord.
1 Thessalonians 4:17

My Class Reunion
Look at yourselves! Look at us!
What do you see?

I see beyond the baldness and the grayness of hair
Or the few facial wrinkles that may have appeared
I see beyond who may have traveled the farthest
Or whom we think have the most money
I see beyond the waistlines
Or the saggy underarms

I see a room of wisdom where once our fate was obscure
I see victory in many aspects of our lives
That each of us, in some form or fashion, had to endure
I feel the warmth of love
And a majestic pride
From whence God blessed us from above
I don't see much regrets and sorrow
I see a legacy of awe and wonder
And positive promises for tomorrow
I see a generation in which we all have contributed much
Yet there is so much we have not begun to touch

I challenge you my classmates to keep a positive image and a
progressive perspective on life
If you should fall, make certain one of us
Reaches down and helps you from your strife
Teach your children, grandchildren now for some
To grasp hold of the torch, and carry it proudly with honor

Rosetta H. Johnson

To work smart, not necessarily hard, obtain as much education as possible
Knowledge is powerful and is the gateway to success
It is our passport to the future
Tomorrow belongs to the people who prepare for it best

I love you, the class of 1971
May you continue to achieve in life
Happiness, love, success, and much, much fun!
Let your evening be an event ever to remember!
This beautiful, cozy night *(29ᵗʰ day)* in the year 2001 of December!

The Excitement

Jesus is an on-time God
He is never too early
And He is never too late
He alone, knows our fate

Only those that have followed His commands
Will be identified with that special 'brand'
What a glorious sight it will be
Home at last, Holy and free

Never concerned about sickness, death or wealth
Having all the riches in glory and excellent health
Laughing and singing on the majestic choir
Responding to Jesus, whatever His desires

Greeting loved ones gone from yester year
Never having to wipe a single tear
The light will be shining so bright that one can clearly see
All the gifts stored in Heaven for you and for me

Needing nothing, everything is there
God's chosen people can shout a jubilant cheer
Hallelujah! Hallelujah!
Praise God, thank you! We are here!

Rosetta H. Johnson

But seek ye first the kingdom of God and His righteousness,
and all these things shall be added unto you.

Matthew 6:33

Seek First God

Stay in the presence of God
Pray continually, seek His face
Cling to Him with your heart
Expect nothing less than His love and grace

He'll give you what you need
Because God always provides
The Earth is the Lord's and all that is within
He only asks that you trust Him and abide

Seek God first and His righteousness
Trust God at His Word
He reigns over you
Your faith He deserves

Fear not, have faith and trust God
What a dreadful scene it would be
To stand before God and be found guilty
And not claim your room in eternity

Our God is exalted high and lifted up as King
He is sovereign over all things
Pray and acknowledge His name in Heaven
Give Him preeminence, give praises to Him and sing

Seek Him first in your life
To God always be humble
All other things will be added to you
He is there, should you stumble

*Take my yoke upon you and learn of me, for I am meek
and lowly in heart, and ye shall find rest unto your
souls. For my yoke is easy and my burden is light.*
Matthew 11:29-30

Don't Worry

God is my provider
All my needs He gives to me
I don't have to worry
I place my hope in only Thee.

Life is more than the food I eat
Or the clothes that are on my back
Worry? Not me
There is nothing that I lack

I cannot add more time to my life
This, only God can control
I refuse to worry
I will praise God and be bold

Does not the Father feed the birds
As they fly, search, and sing
I don't have to worry
All provisions, God will bring

Solomon with all his riches
Was not as beautiful as the lilies in the field
Worry? Not me
God is my armor and my shield

Take time to smell the roses
Seek God first and His righteousness
I don't have to worry because
Strength in the Lord brings me happiness

Do not worry about tomorrow
Tomorrow will take care of itself
Why worry
Leave your worries on *God's Divine Shelf*

Rosetta H. Johnson

Let your light so shine before men that they may see your
good works and glorify your Father which is in heaven.
Matthew 5:16

A Better Me

A Queen of the God most high
More than a conqueror
My God will provide

A positive image, a better me
Potentials overflowing, unrelentless faith
Internal confirmation, flourishing like the sea

The seeds I speak grow strong and healthy
Accepting nothing less than
A future being wealthy

Believing in self, fulfilling my dreams
Failure is not an answer
No matter how difficult it seems

My spiritual walk will continue to grow
In the things I do, the way I act
The service I give to God will show

Great is the Lord, and greatly to be praised;
and his greatness is unsearchable.

Psalms 145:3

God's Greatness

God's greatness, always appreciate
The awesome wonders of this world
Admiring the blue waters and the magic of the sky
Realizing this world is a precious pearl

Be determined to enjoy each moment
Let God's Word embed in your heart
Dare not drift far from Him
His Word will last forever—never to depart

God will always be your strength
Your breastplate of protection
A God whose love showers over you
Displaying a divine spiritual connection

Serve the Lord with gladness; come before
His presence with singing.
Psalm 100:2

An Angel Called to Serve

Even before you were conceived
There was a calling on your life
An angel called to serve
Freeing others from their strife

The joy of the Lord is your strength
Keep a smile upon your face
An angel called to serve
Displaying God's love and His grace

Keep a humble attitude
Reach out your hands and help others
You are an angel called to serve
Treating others like your brothers

Rosetta H. Johnson

Eternal Things

Seek the things of Heaven
Where Christ sits high and looks low
Heaven is a real place
Where we all yearn to go

Put to death those sins lurking within your spirit
You are a Christian, evil desires should not exist
You are a new creature in Christ
Do not allow anger and wrath in your midst

God has chosen you
Handpicked by choice
Live your life to the fullest
Speak out and be God's voice.

I will love thee, O Lord, my strength. The Lord is my rock and my fortress and my deliverer; my God, my strength, in whom I will trust; my buckler and the horn of my salvation, and my high tower.

Psalm 18:1-2

Inner Strength

If the Lord is with us
We can do anything
All our burdens and sorrows
To Him, He invites us to bring

Rely on your inner strength
Be not dismayed or despair
Keep your spirit uplifted
Lean on the Lord, He cares

Rosetta H. Johnson

Rely on God's Strength

Stay in strength with God
God has chosen you as His own
Delight in the Word of God
Eventually, you will enjoy a new home

Trust in the Lord with all your heart
Lean not to your own understanding
Open up your heart and receive Him
This is what the Lord is commanding

Delight yourself in the Lord
Dwell on spiritual thoughts in pleasure
Intimately seeking to satisfy God
Your rewards you cannot measure

The Lord continues to give you strength
Your body, He has fortified
He is a keeper of His word
Everything you need He will supply

> *Ye are of God, little children, and have overcome them; because*
> *greater is he that is in you, than he that is in the world.*
>
> ### 1 John 4:4

Memories

As I look toward the future
Reminiscing about the past
Living in the present
Enjoying memories that will last

Life is like a bed of roses
Beautiful flowers with thorns along the way
Learn to appreciate its beauty
And never let obstacles cloud your day

Life will bring you your share of bruises
And you will experience disappointments, too
Expect a life full of excitement
Because greater is He that is in you

Praying Unceasingly

God will always hear our prayers
If we truly show we love His name
Always praying to Him sincerely
Never expecting fortune or fame

Loving God is really easy
He does not ask anything extra of His heirs
He only asks that we love Him only
In return, our burdens He will bear

That is not much to ask of us
He is the mighty and awesome Savior
He alone sacrificed his life
We continue to ask for his favor

Rosetta H. Johnson

God's Glory

God's glory is displayed by the whole body
He is the head of the church we worship
Being together with God's people
We relish the beauty of his friendship

We gather together to tell of God's glory
Seeking to meet God face to face
Singing, dancing, displaying the story
At the right time and in the right place

What are you giving to help God's ministry
Are you setting examples for others to follow
Planting seeds and nourishing them daily
Letting your heart cry, showing true sorrow

The Spirit itself beareth witness with our spirit, that we are the children of God, and if children, then heirs of God, and joint heirs with Christ, if so be that we suffer with him, that we may be also glorified together.

Romans 8:16-17

God's Ambassador

I have disobeyed you Lord
Reconcile me to your heart
I have offended you in so many ways
Don't let go of me, else I will fall apart

What good is it for me to gain the world
And my soul is left out on bay
I pledged to be your ambassador
Just lead me along life's narrow way

I am a joint heir with you, Christ
Let me claim my rightful place
Having peace within, I am not afraid
Preparing to meet you face to face

Rosetta H. Johnson

The Armor of God

Abide under the shadow of the Almighty
Wear God's armor of shield for protection
God will never leave or forsake you
Stay under his fold with a holy connection

You were one of the few that was chosen
From the many that were called
He made you a captain in his army
God is the Commander-in-Chief, you cannot fall

Be a soldier in God's army
The battle has already been fought
March in step with Jesus
Obey what He has taught

Take with you the helmet of salvation
And the sword in your hand
Beckon to His every call
Respond only to God's commands

Never concerned about tomorrow
Living just for today
Looking into the future
Is much too far away

Preparing now to be ready
For that day when Jesus calls your name
When you stand before Him on judgment
You alone will be to blame

> *I therefore the prisoner of the Lord beseech you that ye walk worthy of the vocation wherewith which you were called.*
>
> ***Ephesians 4:1***

Prisoner

There was a time in my life
When my soul was bound for hell
Since I accepted Jesus
My soul is now well

God gives me the comfort of His love
His mercy has forgiven me of sinning
I have consolation in Christ
I am on the team that is winning

I am a prisoner of the Lord's
Walking worthy of His calling
With all lowliness and gentleness
God will prevent me from falling

He will not let me deceive myself
Thinking that I am something
In God's sight, I am weak and lowly
This amounts to almost nothing

Seeking to have a spiritual relationship
That will exemplify my love for Christ
Displaying a meek and humble spirit
Manifesting a Christian-filled life

Rosetta H. Johnson

Have mercy upon me, O God, according to thy loving kindness, according unto the multitude of thy tender mercies, blot out my transgressions. Wash me thoroughly from my iniquity, and cleanse me from my sins.

Psalm 51:1-2

Cleansed

I know I serve a forgiving God
Forgive me Lord, for I want to feel clean
Let my countenance have a glow like Moses
Where my face will shine and gleam

Cleanse me so I can be cleaned
Wash me whiter than snow
I will show my gratitude for your mercy
With a thankful heart, wherever I may go

All that I have hoped for, you provided
And all my needs, you always supplied
Standing on all your promises
Leaning on your shoulders as my personal guide

Then he said unto them, "Go your way, eat the fat and drink
the sweet, and send portions unto them for whom nothing
is prepared; for this day is holy unto our Lord, neither
be ye sorry, for the joy of the Lord is your strength."
Nehemiah 8:10

Divine Strength

The joy of the Lord is your strength
Your inner smile will not change
God made our bodies the temple for the Holy Spirit
The world has no power to come in and rearrange

Keep me ever always mindful
Of the love you have for me
How you bled, died and suffered
Upon the cross at Calvary

A painful death that must have been
Never uttering an unpleasant word
Watching the sinful actions of the people
Must have made your heart disturbed

Rosetta H. Johnson

As the hart panteth after the water brooks, so
panteth my soul after thee, O God.
Psalm 42:1

A Fresh Start

I need a fresh start
Begin with a review of my heart
No more excuses for my failures in the past
Pressing towards the mark where my journey will last

Acting in faith
Being careful how I think
I am the missing part
That needed extra link

Keeping my heart with all diligence
For out of it springs the issues of life
Walking in the footsteps of Jesus Christ
Avoiding all unnecessary strife

Prayer, faith and the Word of God
Are all powerful tools
Walking the Christian journey
Abiding by the rules

Living for Jesus

God is not impressed with your eloquent prayers
He looks within your heart and knows how much you care
God is not interested in your large congregation
He is more interested in how many received salvation

Present your bodies a living sacrifice
Be transformed by renewing your minds
Practice living the Word as God instructed
Eternal life has been promised to all mankind

God knows everything about us
He sees our every walk
He even knows our motives and our every thought
The things we do and the way we talk

Listen carefully and rejoice
One by one, God will call your name
If it is written in the Lamb's Book of Life
Proudly step forward and make your claim

Rosetta H. Johnson

Blessed is the man that walketh not in the counsel
of the ungodly, nor standeth in the way of sinners,
nor sitteth in the seat of the scornful.
Psalm 1:1

Walking Vessel

Let me be that walking vessel
To show others God through me
Applying the spiritual gifts that have been given
Knowing the entire world will be able to see

Treating others like I want to be treated
Loving my neighbors like I want to be loved
Charity starts within my heart
Written examples have been given from above

Yielding willingly to the Spirit
Walking cautiously in the path given
Listening carefully to what He says
Trying not to do the things that are forbidden

I press toward the mark for the prize of the
high calling of God in Christ Jesus.
Philippians 3:14

Keep Pressing On

Faith is the substance of things hoped for
The evidence of things not seen
Rid your heart of all malice
And keep your thoughts clean

All your sins have been forgiven
And there is a place in Heaven waiting for you
Keep pressing toward the mark
God will bring you all the way through

God said He will never leave you
And all your burdens He said He will bear
He is a God who keeps His promises
Cast all your cares upon Him and leave them there

Rosetta H. Johnson

> *In whom we have redemption through His blood the*
> *forgiveness of sins according to the riches of His grace.*
>
> ***Ephesians 1:7***

A Second Chance

I may not have been given the honor
Of reaching fame on Earth
I know I was predestined to become
What I am, from the beginning of my birth

You are the portion of food I need
To sustain my daily life
Let your Word pierce my heart
Like a sharp, two-edged knife

Jesus is the vine
I am His branch
An intimate relationship we have
He gave me a second chance

I know first-hand of your precious work
I know because you did it for me
You alone died on Calvary
Because of this I have been made free

I will always share your story
Throughout this vast land
Use me as your disciple
Continue to hold my hand

Confess your faults one to another, and pray for one another, that ye may be healed. The effectual, fervent prayer of a righteous man availeth much.

James 5:16

God's Healing Hands

You said you are ill
The doctor has not given you any hope
Keep trusting in Jesus
Believe only His report

God didn't give you a spirit of fear
But one of hope, love and a good mind
Remember the power of Jesus
God's healing hands are always on time

We serve a God who has never failed
Do not worry and do not fret
Wait on the Lord and be of good cheer
His healing hands will touch you yet

Smile delightful in Jesus
He will always be near
Trust Him, He knows your needs
He listens and He hears your prayers

Rosetta H. Johnson

Cast me not away from thy presence; and
take not thy holy spirit from me.
Psalm 51:11

Everlasting Glory

The grass withers, the flower fades
God's glory is revealed
Out of God's mercy, He protects us
The invisible God will never be sealed

The glory of the gospel of Jesus Christ
Is intended to be known to all
Do not profess to be wise
And instead, from His grace, you fall

Behold the glory of God
Cry out admitting you are nothing but grass
Let His abiding words comfort you
The Word of God will last

You are helpless without the Lord
Do not let go of His hands
Keep yourself deeply grounded and rooted in His Word
Asking Him to make you part of the Master's Plan

Put your trust in God
The things of the world will pass away
You can think about tomorrow
But plan only for today

The Word of God will live forever
God's Word will always stand
His Word will be fulfilled
Trust and believe, follow His command

Captain Carla Renee Johnson

Do not think of this mission as a lemon
Consider all the mixtures you can use
Sip on it like lemonade
Take pride in the attitude you choose

Remember God is omnipresent
And His presence is everywhere
He only asks that you be faithful
He will answer your every prayer

Take your tour as an opportunity
To explore the beautiful world God has made
God sends His traveling angels with you
There is no need to be afraid

God said fear not, for I am with you
Believe His words, for they are true
They were not written for Jesus
But for sinners like me and you

You truly are an angel called to serve
Helping others in their distress
God said He will never leave you or forsake you
Lean on the Savior—you have passed the test

As you fly above the blue sky
Thousands of miles away from home
God is in the midst of everything
You understand, you are not alone

Where God leads you, He will follow
Listen attentively and let Him be your guide
Follow the route God has chosen
Rest assured He is by your side

Let your mind reflect on Heaven
Do not become fretful or be dismayed
The Lord is your light and salvation
He will keep and protect you everyday

The tears I may shed shows my selfishness
Always wanting to keep you near
I know you have a special calling, Go!
Serve our country; I will keep you in constant prayer

Call me everyday now
I simply want to hear your voice
Knowing that you are okay
Will make me smile and jubilantly rejoice

We serve a merciful and loving God
He sits high and looks low
He watches over us constantly
Guiding our footsteps wherever we may go

God always shows His presence
He neither slumbers nor sleeps
God told us in His own words
That our souls, He will always keep

The Lord is your shepherd
No need to ever be in fear
The wall that God has built around you
Will keep any harm from coming near

Rosetta H. Johnson

You are a champion in your own right
Always know that you are loved
Not only by your family
But from your Heavenly Father above

Think about home
But do not become homesick
You were not only chosen
But you were carefully handpicked

Young lady, little girl, my sweetheart
One of the chosen few
I blow a kiss from afar
Asking God to always be with you

Wisdom

Listen closely to God's teachings
Learn common sense and don't turn away
Biblical knowledge will make you wise
Nourish your spirit, do not go astray

Love wisdom, don't reject wisdom
The best thing about wisdom is wisdom herself
Good sense is more important
Than anything else you may possess

Value wisdom and hold tightly to her
Like a queen wearing her crown
You will be admired with great honors
Keep smiling, never showing a grimace frown

Listen and obey God's teachings
Feast on eternal things that will last
Your roads will not be blocked
Do not stray from the narrow path

Free From Worry

I serve a powerful and mighty God
A God who sits high and looks low
He is a God that neither sleeps nor slumbers
He watches over me wherever I may go

He is a God that is true to His words
Many promises He has made to me
I never doubt or question His actions
His death has set my captive soul free

Jesus is my best friend
Everything we always share
Free from stress or heavy burdens
I have given to Jesus for Him to bear

There is nothing too difficult for God to handle
He is the creator with the Master's Plan
I am less than a dew drop on a flower
God holds the world in the palm of His hands

In the midst of my self-pity
God's voice will speak within
Remember, I died, suffered and bore your pains
I am the only God you must proclaim

But they that wait upon the Lord shall renew their strength;
they shall mount up with wings as eagles, they shall run,
and not be weary; and they shall walk and not faint.
Isaiah 40:31

Run After God

Run after God!
Cling to Him with your whole heart
Pray continually; don't worry
Only God can heal a broken heart

God will give you what you need
All our needs God said He would provide
Accept God for who He is
Just trust Him and He will abide

Run after God!
Intensely run the race
Seek Him first and His righteousness
One day, you will meet Him face to face

Rosetta H. Johnson

For all flesh is as grass, and all the glory of man as the flower
of grass. The grass withereth, and the flower thereof falleth
away; But the word of the Lord endureth forever. And this
is the word which by the gospel is preached unto you.

1 Peter 1:24-25

Jesus is Real

In times of despair
God is always there
If in doubt about what to do
Pray to God, let Him walk you through

You have come too far, don't quit now
Do not let this world make you feel discouraged
Think of the precious gifts stored for you in Heaven
God's love will keep you focused and encouraged

Keep your eyes lifted unto the hills
Knowing all your help comes from He
Who keeps all His promises
Fulfilling them for you and me

Jesus truly is real!
Pray to God in your secret place
He knows exactly how you feel
He will keep you with His saving grace

My Love for God

Let your love and loyalty to God
Be written deeply in your mind
Embracing the greatest love ever given
Jesus, Himself, sacrificed for all mankind

God and people will love you dearly
They will consider you a success
Trust in the Lord with all your heart
Giving God your very best

Let God lead you
Follow Him and believe
Honor God and give Him what He requires
You will receive more than you will need

Ask God for wisdom and understanding
They are more valuable than silver or gold
Wisdom will bring you a long life, wealth and honor
The secrets of Heaven will He unfold

Use common sense and sound judgment
They will help you live a long and flourishing life
You can walk safely and not stumble
Rest peacefully without strife

Don't be afraid of sudden disasters
The Lord will protect you from all harm
Though storms may strike many others
You stay focused; don't be alarmed

Rosetta H. Johnson

The Lord is in His Holy place
Looking down from Heaven above
He is a keeper of His word
He takes care of all He loves

And take the helmet of salvation, and the sword

of the Spirit, which is the word of God.

Ephesians 6:17

Always Protected

Let the angels swing the swords
From the left and the right
Not allowing the adversary to enter
Neither day or at night

Abiding in the shadow of the Almighty
Listening to His beckoning call
Building a shield around you
No danger entering through the walls

Keeping a sound mind
Expressing a cheerful heart
Using the grace God has given
Basking in His presence each day as it starts

Seeing the mighty works of His hands
Listening eagerly to His voice
Enjoying peace within your heart
Worshiping Jesus, is your choice

Always studying to show thyself approved
Not focusing on things from the past
Build your faith on the solid rock
Knowing what you do for God will last

Verily I say unto you, whosoever shall not receive the kingdom
of God as a little child shall in no wise enter therein.
Luke 18:17

The Child Within

I pray for a happy heart
As well as a cheerful mind
Speaking words of encouragement
Showing love to all mankind

Being lighthearted and laughing more
Letting laughter be medicine to my soul
Allowing it to heal internally
While stressful thoughts begin to unfold

Enjoying life like little children
Making games of everything
Leaving my burdens at the altar
God said to Him we should bring

Letting the playful child within me
Flow freely like the breeze of the wind
Feeling safe and secure like a child
Knowing I am protected by my Friend

Rosetta H. Johnson

For a thousand years in thy sight are but as yesterday
when it is past, and as a watch in the night.

Psalms 90:4

God's Time

In moments of your distress
Place your thoughts on God and rest
This trial is only a little test
Continue to praise God and be blessed

Let your quiet time with God be precious
Read His word and meditate
In His time He will work things out
His response is never too early or too late

God knows what is best for us
After all, He is the Creator of this great universe
Only He can give the command
Be patient, it is all in the Master's hand

Worrying will not change anything
Stress and headaches—that is all it brings
God has everything in control
He is our Lord, the sovereign King

Go ye therefore, and teach all nations, baptizing them in the name of the Father, and of the Son, and of the Holy Ghost.

Matthew 28:19

Share the Gospel

I want to know you better
Telling others of your grace
Knowing there is none other
Who could ever take your place

Showing evidence of my salvation
Sharing the gospel to others I meet
Holding up the name of Jesus
To everyone I am privileged to greet

Rosetta H. Johnson

But ye are a chosen generation, a royal priesthood, an holy nation,
a peculiar people; that ye should show forth the praises of Him
who hath called you out of darkness into His marvelous light.

1 Peter 2:9

I Am Different

Let my actions reflect my faith
Sacrificing myself in love
Exhorting God in Heaven above

Let God's light shine through me
So the good works done
Others will clearly see

Let me stand out from the crowd
No more pretenses to impress
But speaking your Word boldly to express

Let me please you God
Being saved and glorifying you
Making a positive difference in all that I do

Not conforming to the world around me
But living a quality life
Free from worry, heartaches or strife

You therefore, beloved seeing ye know these things before, beware lest ye also, being led away with the error of the wicked, fall from your steadfastness. But grow in grace, and in the knowledge of our Lord and Saviour Jesus Christ. To him be glory both now and for ever.

2 Peter 3: 17-18

Growing In Grace

Let the fruit in you show that you are like Christ
Growing in the grace and knowledge of the Savior
In the words you speak, deeds you do and a loving heart
Conscientious of your conduct and constant behavior

The heavens will pass away
As the Lord will come as a thief in the night
The elements will melt with a fervent heat
Blessed be the Lord, oh what an awesome sight

Striving to manifest an exceptional lifestyle
That is Holy and acceptable in God's sight
Being obedient to His word
Like a bright star shining through the night

Expecting eternal rest and joy with God
Looking for a new Heaven and a new Earth
In which only righteousness and holiness dwell
Forever free from eternal damnation known to all as hell

Work with a sense of urgency
Knowing Jesus may come or call today
Doing things that will count for eternity
Expecting Jesus to come any day

Rosetta H. Johnson

Jesus will find you personally
You are precious and special to Him
Let Him find you diligently doing His will
With a sweet melody of music in your heart as you sing

Let not your heart be troubled
In Jesus Christ the Lord you believe
He will give you peace and understanding
Open your heart and all His blessing receive

There Is a Time

To everything there is a season
No need to question if there is a reason

A time for every purpose
Accept things as they surface

A time to kill and a time to heal
Keep praying to God, He knows how you feel

A time to break down and a time to build up
God alone will fill your cup

There is also a time to weep
God said our sinful souls He will keep

There is a time to laugh and a time to mourn
God knew everything about us before we were born

There is also a time to dance
You are promised that second chance

There is a time to cast away stones and a time to gather stones
Walking with Jesus, you are never alone

A time to gain and a time to lose
It is left up to Jesus whomever He choose

There is a time to keep and a time to throw away
Salvation is promised, accept Jesus today

Rosetta H. Johnson

A time to rend and a time to sew
Praise God always, our blessings flow

A time to keep silent and a time to speak
The God we serve makes strong the weak

A time to love and a time to hate
Only God knows our eternal fate

A time of war and a time of peace
Blessed be the one whose soul rests in peace

The Presence of God

I can see your presence everywhere
In the fluffy clouds as they move through the sky
In the whirlwind as sand lifts up in the air

I can feel your presence everywhere
In your Word that I read
And in all your good deeds

I can hear your presence everywhere
In the chirp of a bird sitting on a tree branch
In the laughter of a child playing very near

I can smell your presence everywhere
From the sweet aroma of the blooming flowers
Drawing me closer to you every hour

I can taste your presence everywhere
It is sweeter than the honey in the honeycombs
To love you more is my solemn prayer

Rosetta H. Johnson

Create in me a clean heart, O God, and renew a right spirit within me. Cast me not away from thy presence, and take not thy Holy Spirit from me.

Psalms 51:10-11

A Heart As Pure As Gold

Lord I beg you not to depart from me
Never ever become my enemy
For you alone hold my destiny
Your dying on Calvary has made me free
Make my heart as pure as gold.

You are the only one my soul truly loves
Knowing you makes me love you more and more
You know my inner thoughts and how I feel
Forgive me, if the Holy Spirit ever I have grieved
My heart, make it pure as gold.

I beg you to keep your presence near
Remove all doubt and any fear
I am yours, a vessel you can use
Heavenly bound, you I will not refuse
Keep my heart as pure as gold.